When
Helping
Heals

**Tracy Kuperus and
Roland Hoksbergen**

CALVIN SHORTS

Calvin PRESS

COLLEGE

Grand Rapids, MI • calvin.edu/press

Published 2016 by the Calvin College Press
3201 Burton St. SE
Grand Rapids, MI 49546

Publisher's Cataloging-in-Publication data
Names: Kuperus, Tracy, author. | Hoksbergen, Roland G., author.
Title: When helping heals / by Tracy Kuperus and Roland Hoksbergen.
Series: Calvin Shorts.
Description: Includes bibliographical references. | Grand Rapids, MI: Calvin College Press, 2016.
Identifiers: ISBN 978-1-937555-21-4 (pbk.) | 978-1-937555-22-1 (ebook) | LCCN 2016957109
Subjects: LCC Economic development--Moral and ethical aspects. | Economic development projects--Moral and ethical aspects. | Economic development projects--Developing countries. | Globalization--|Moral and ethical aspects. | International business enterprises--Religious aspects--Christianity. | Social service--Religious aspects--Christianity. | Nonprofit organizations--Moral and ethical aspects. | Non-governmental organizations--Moral and ethical aspects. | BISAC BUSINESS & ECONOMICS / Development / Economic Development | BUSINESS & ECONOMICS / Nonprofit Organizations & Charities / General | POLITICAL SCIENCE / NGOs (Non-Governmental Organizations) | POLITICAL SCIENCE / Globalization | SOCIAL SCIENCE / Developing & Emerging Countries | SOCIAL SCIENCE / Philanthropy & Charity
Classification: LCC HD73 .K87 2016 | DDC 338.9--dc23

Cover design: Robert Alderink
Interior design and typeset: Katherine Lloyd, The DESK

Contents

Acknowledgments

The authors wish to thank colleagues Daniel Miller, David Bronkema, and Amy Patterson for reviewing early drafts and making helpful suggestions, the spring 2016 introductory class on International Development for all their feedback, Calvin Shorts editor Susan Felch for her countless wise editorial suggestions, and the Nagel Institute for World Christianity for its financial support.

Series Editor's Foreword

Midway along the journey of our life
I woke to find myself in some dark woods,
For I had wandered off from the straight path.

So begins the *Divine Comedy*, a classic meditation on the Christian life, written by Dante Alighieri in the fourteenth century.

Dante's three images—a journey, a dark forest, and a perplexed pilgrim—still feel familiar today, don't they?

We can readily imagine our own lives as a series of journeys, not just the big journey from birth to death, but also all the little trips from home to school, from school to job, from place to place, from old friends to new. In fact, we often feel we are simultaneously on multiple journeys that tug us in diverse and sometimes opposing directions. We recognize those dark woods from fairy tales and nightmares and the all-too-real conundrums that crowd our everyday lives. No wonder we frequently feel perplexed. We wake up shaking our heads, unsure if we know how to live wisely today or tomorrow or next week.

This series has in mind just such perplexed pilgrims. Each book invites you, the reader, to walk alongside experienced guides who will help you understand the contours of the road as well as the surrounding landscape. They will cut back the underbrush, untangle myths and misconceptions, and suggest ways to move forward.

And they will do it in books intended to be read in an evening or during a flight. Calvin Shorts are designed not just for perplexed pilgrims, but also for busy ones. We live in a complex and changing world. We need nimble ways to acquire knowledge, skills, and wisdom. These books are one way to meet those needs.

John Calvin, after whom this series is named, recognized our pilgrim condition. "We are always on the road," he said, and although this road, this life, is full of perplexities, it is also "a gift of divine kindness which is not to be refused." Calvin Shorts takes as its starting point this claim that we are called to live well in a world that is both gift and challenge.

In the *Divine Comedy*, Dante's guide is Virgil, a wise but not omniscient mentor. So too, the authors in the Calvin Shorts series don't pretend to know it all. They, like you and me, are pilgrims. And they invite us to walk with them as together we seek to live more faithfully in this world that belongs to God.

Susan M. Felch
Executive Editor
The Calvin College Press

Additional Resources

Additional online resources for *When Helping Heals* may be available at http://www.calvin.edu/press.

Additional information, references, and citations are included in the notes at the end of this book. Rather than using footnote numbers, these comments are keyed to phrases and page numbers.

Should We Help People in the Global South?

1

Calvin College's semester program in Ghana, which both of us have directed, is exciting and challenging at the same time; exciting because it is so incredibly new and different, and challenging for virtually the same reasons. Among the first activities we schedule is a trip to Northern Ghana where students interact with Ghanaian farmers who are struggling against great odds on land that is too dry and not very fertile. In small mud homes, we talk with families whose lives are hard. We visit schools where children pack into crowded classrooms of fifty pupils or more. We can't help but notice that all too often there are no pencils or paper in the rooms. When the visit ends, we file into our air-conditioned bus and get out our smart phones to check the latest news on social media. We feel that something isn't right.

Together we begin to think and talk about what we have seen, because these are hard realities. Students wonder, "What's going on here? Why is there so much inequality in our world? Where is God in all this?" They also ask, "What can we do?"

As Christians who care deeply about the well-being of God's children throughout the world, we have learned that answers to all of these questions are very important, but they are also complex. Together, we have been working for more than sixty-five combined years to come up with good answers, especially to the question of what we can do.

A good place to start addressing these questions is to notice that things have actually been getting better. People often say that the poor are getting poorer, but the truth is that much progress has been made recently to reduce poverty. In 1990, 50 percent of the world's people lived in extreme poverty. Today the figure is down to 14 percent. Almost ninety-three of every one thousand children born in 1990 died before they were five. Now the figure is down to forty-three. In the last twenty-five years, 2.6 billion people have obtained access to safe drinking water.

Of course there is still a long way to go before everyone has the chance to live the full life that God intends for his people. Even after the gains, over 800 million people still go hungry every day. 30 million people, many of them children, are held as slaves. 60 million refugees have no safe place to be. 150 million children have no real home and live their lives on the streets instead. Though progress has been made, this is no time to rest.

As with our students studying in Ghana, a normal Christian response to these realities is a desire to help, a desire strengthened by the two great commandments – "Love the Lord your God with all your heart and with all your soul and with all your strength and with all your mind," and "Love your neighbor as yourself" (Luke 10:27). How can we love neighbors in need if we don't help them? As 1 John 3:17 says, "If anyone has material possessions and sees a brother or sister in need but has no pity on them, how can the love of God be in that person?" Many Christians are drawn to the story of the Good Samaritan. The story is so striking because the Samaritan reaches across cultural and religious lines to help his neighbor in a time of great distress. Jesus says that if we meet the needs of people who are hungry, thirsty, refugees, without clothing, sick, or in prison, we are extending our hands to Jesus himself (Matt. 25:34-40). Christians hear these stories and recognize that we are called to help those in need.

This is where the difficulties often begin. We want to help, but we have doubts, too. First, we wonder how addressing physical needs fits with Christian beliefs that focus more on saving souls for eternity than on padding nests in the here and now. Why is fighting hunger and poverty important when where someone will spend eternity is what's really on the line?

If we agree that God calls us to care about people's lives in this world, we encounter a second set of questions. Are those of us from the rich countries of the world really capable of providing assistance to the world's poor? Maybe we will focus too much on material goods and ignore other important parts of people's lives like dignity, cultural integrity, and a sense of belonging. Maybe we have a false sense of superiority, perhaps even "savior complexes," that keep us from connecting with people in other countries in helpful ways.

In fact, we are hit with a steady stream of messages

telling us we don't really know how to help people. Many recent books argue that when we try to help, we are really causing harm. How? First, our efforts at assistance may lead to dependence instead of self-sufficiency. Second, our money may foster corruption at all levels of society. Third, assistance from the outside may create and nurture structures that favor the powerful over the less powerful. These arguments leave us with two basic questions: If we want to help, can we? And do we know how?

Recent Christian authors have picked up on these themes as well. Two influential books are *When Helping Hurts* (2009) by Steve Corbett and Brian Fikkert and Robert Lupton's *Toxic Charity* (2012). It is not that these Christians think we shouldn't care. In fact, they believe God calls us to help our neighbors. But when they look out over the assistance strategies of the last decades, they see a lot of failure. Because they emphasize these failures, their readers may also fall into despair. Corbett and Fikkert acknowledge this reality in the second edition of their book.

> Unfortunately, we have also heard some readers of the first edition say that they are not quite sure what to do next. They want to "help without hurting," but they are not sure how to get started. Some have even said that they feel a bit paralyzed, being so worried about doing harm that they are afraid to do anything at all. And in a few rare but

disturbing cases, some have used the first edition to argue – erroneously – that nothing should be done to help people who are poor, as all efforts are likely to do harm.

A careful reading of their book reveals many wonderful ideas about how to help our neighbors. For many, however, the main message they hear is how hard helping really is.

The story we tell in *When Helping Heals* does not ignore the failures of international development and foreign aid but focuses on the successes too, and especially on what we have learned over the years. Like Corbett and Fikkert, we know that God intends for us to help our neighbors, and we want to learn how to do a better job. In this book, we will talk about the short term assistance needed in dire situations like natural disasters or famines. But we will also include some of the big lessons we've learned about how to foster and build just, peaceful, and prosperous societies that allow everyone to flourish.

Often our first instinct in a disaster situation is to send people exactly what they seem to need at that moment: money, food, water, and clothing. When we look at long term development, however, the best community and national assistance strategies are often different. We may need to invest in education and job training or lend money for start-up businesses. We may need to work toward reconciliation in times of conflict, hold government and business leaders accountable, fight corruption, and promote social justice. We may need to organize community groups, advocate for certain economic policies, and work to build just legal systems. As with physical illness, the remedy must correspond to the sickness. If we apply the wrong medicine, we are likely to cause harm instead of healing. We need to understand the problems if we are going to find effective cures. This takes work, but the benefits are great.

Before we get too much further, let's clarify a few terms. All terms that appear in boldface are included in the glossary at the end of this book. **International development** is a process of change that seeks to overcome poverty and injustice and promote health, education, social well-being, and a generally flourishing society in the **Global South**. International development work involves intentional efforts to move development forward. Such efforts include the sorts of tasks noted in the previous paragraph and can be done by foreigners from the **Global North** or by people who live in the Global South. International development work is often supported by **foreign aid**, which refers to money given to countries to promote their development. Foreign aid can be provided to a country bilaterally, when one country supplies funds directly to another country, or multilaterally, when aid is funneled to a country through a global institution like the **World Bank** or the United Nations.

With these definitions as a backdrop, we review the

ways international development work has been conducted over time. We focus on how foreign aid and various assistance strategies have contributed to international development. We approach this study as Christians who live in a world where governments and many organizations are secular. We consider what Christian organizations are doing on their own, but also how Christians interact with secular development programs. Finally, we draw some key lessons and tell some stories about successful development work.

We begin in chapter 2 by looking at the long shadow of **colonialism** in the Global South. In chapters 3 and 4, we trace the history of development from the end of World War II to the present. Based on this history, we ask in chapter 5 what we have learned and whether we really can play a healing role. In chapter 6, we review some current trends in international development work. In chapter 7, we tell stories of two exemplary Christian organizations, one working in Bangladesh and the other in Honduras. Our concluding chapter offers words of encouragement and hope.

In this short book, we cannot offer a complete analysis of how helping heals. But we hope to make a good start in reinforcing a positive view of how we can engage more faithfully and helpfully with our neighbors around the world.

The Impact of Colonialism on Our World Today

2

The world today is divided between what is called the Global North (relatively rich, politically stable, and powerful states) and the Global South (relatively poor, less stable, and formerly colonized states). A few countries like Brazil, China, and India lie in between, sometimes referred to as Newly Industrializing Countries, emerging markets, or even BRICs (for Brazil, Russia, India, China).

The history of continuous Global North and Global South interaction began with the Portuguese and Spanish exploration of the Americas in the fifteenth century. Over the next five hundred years, European nations colonized almost every country in South and Central America, Asia, the Middle East, and Africa. Today, these countries constitute the Global South. It is hard to overestimate the impact of colonialism on our world and on the relationships among countries. We would like to draw attention to a few themes from this era that help us understand how the Global North and Global South relate to one another. First, colonialism was a disaster for most people in the Global South. It empowered and enriched a few but marginalized and impoverished the majority. It doesn't matter if the colonizers were motivated by status, political power, economic gain, or Christian mission because those who were colonized still saw colonialism as conquest, domination, and exploitation. **Indigenous peoples** were not asked what they wanted or needed; they were imposed upon.

In many ways, colonialism laid the groundwork for the poverty that many Global South countries experience today. Colonialism led to national boundaries that today still cause ethnic divisions and conflicts. It created elitist, centralized, and authoritarian governments. Colonizers destroyed local institutions and paid little attention to promoting democracy. They structured economies in ways that benefitted their imperial power. The resulting trade patterns and transportation networks continue to define Global South countries. These countries often have limited access to the world economy. Local industry is not supported, and traditional agriculture is neglected. Some countries have developed what is called a "**dual economy**," one for those lucky enough to be well-connected to the global economy and the other for those who struggle to make it in a neglected local economy. All these economic issues stem from colonialism. Finally, colonizers disrupted the Global South's social environment. They imposed European languages, introduced European-centered education, and undermined traditional belief systems.

Beyond these physical and institutional changes is another, even deeper consequence of the colonial era. Colonized people changed how they saw and thought of themselves, in ways related to their self-esteem, identity, and worldview. As one scholar points out, the Europeans believed "in the essential cultural differences and superiority of European peoples." They saw their subjects as inferior, primitive, and backward. It was the Europeans' moral duty, by force if necessary, to replace indigenous cultures with a modernized European culture. Many colonized people collapsed under this racial pressure. They also began to believe that European culture was superior to their own. One reason why colonialism lasted so long is that both the colonizers and the colonized adopted a European worldview and identity. Today, we appropriately reject this superior-inferior hierarchy, but it is hard to deny that it remains an underlying current.

Did anything good result from the world's experience with colonialism? As we look back, the answer to this question is a qualified yes. European public health measures improved life expectancy in the colonies. New schools brought impressive educational advancements, first for a few and then gradually for many more. New ways of thinking challenged superstitious ideas, for example, assuming that the birth of twins is a sign of evil. And there were some advances in gender relations, like discouraging the practice of polygamy.

What about the introduction of Christianity, a faith that today dominates in both sub-Saharan Africa and Latin America? What was Christianity's balance sheet during the colonial era?

Christians were most active during the colonial years as foreign missionaries. Christians felt it was their special responsibility to bring the gospel message to the world and to "make disciples of all the nations" (Matt. 28:19–20). Churches and missionary societies in the West sent thousands of missionaries around the world. They wanted to evangelize and civilize the people they thought of as "heathens." By and large, the missionary relationship with colonialism was cooperative and mutually support- ive. Sometimes missionaries followed the colonizers and were pleased that colonial rule allowed them the opportu- nity to evangelize. Other times the missionaries went first and actually encouraged their home countries to colonize a region so they could bring order, peace, and material progress.

Though there were exceptions, most Christians supported colonialism. Missionaries contributed to devel- opment with their evangelistic, medical, and educational work. They often improved the lives of indigenous peo- ple physically and sometimes politically. But the fact of the matter is that the overwhelming majority of Chris- tian missionaries never challenged either the institutions or practices of colonialism. Like most Europeans, they believed that Western advances in science, technology, economics, politics, civic life, and culture were obviously superior to anything else the world had to offer. They thought that spreading these advances to peoples they considered to be primitive and heathen could hardly be anything but good. Christian resistance to colonialism was limited to its worst evils, slavery being one example.

Today most Christian missionaries from the Global

North no longer engage with Christians in the Global South like they did in colonial times. But it is worth asking, as many secular critics do, how many of our modern efforts may actually be a new form of colonialism. Are the **Millennium Development Goals (MDGs)** of the United Nations or short term mission trips to the Global South replicating the colonial goal of civilizing "backward peoples"? To answer this question, read on!

Modernization
and its
Challenges
(1950s-1970s)

3

CHOOSING A PATH
IN THE SHADOW OF THE COLD WAR

It is not totally fair to use the word "development" when we talk about the colonial period. The word was little used before World War II, but became an important concept in the mid-1940s and 1950s. In part, this was the result of two major changes in the world. First, Europe's colonies began their drives for independence. One by one as the colonies broke ties with their colonial masters, they joined ranks with other Global South countries whose independence had come earlier, in particular the states of Latin America. These countries became known as the "**Third World**," a term roughly equivalent to the Global South. The "First World" was thought of as the capitalist West, and the "Second World" was the communist East. Third World countries were economically poorer than countries in either the First or Second Worlds, and they were not aligned with either. Newly independent Third World countries were left to their own devices in a world that had been ordered by the rich states and was structured to favor them. The challenges they faced were daunting, but hopes were high that these countries could develop on their own.

The transition from colonies to independent states was a momentous change, both for these countries and for Western Europe and North America. Rich countries could no longer conquer, dominate, and subject their former colonies. The First World had to see the Third World as a region whose people were not only human (sadly, this was a question in the colonial era), but also global citizens with rights. These rights were codified in the 1948 Universal Declaration of Human Rights. True, colonial powers gave up their power and attitudes reluctantly and gradually, but in the end they could not hold back the tides of change. Those who really did want to help moved in the direction of enabling Third World countries to take their rightful place in the world.

This goal was not easy to achieve, however, because the newly liberated countries faced a second major change. The world had become **bipolar**. The Western First World promoted liberal democracy and **capitalism**. The Second World, dominated by the Soviet Union (USSR), encouraged **communism**, an economic system in which production and prices are managed by the government. Some of the new Third World states hoped they really could be independent and unaligned, but in reality they had to make a choice. The First and Second Worlds were engaged in an economic and geopolitical competition. Third World states often played the role of pawns in this international chess match. They had to pick which side they were going to be on and which system they would adopt. It was a dangerous game that fostered political instability and many wars. These conflicts were caused as much by external meddling as by internal conditions.

The struggle between the First and Second Worlds over who had the better overall political and economic system had a major effect on Third World countries. In part, the "better" system was the one more likely to help countries in the Global South quickly become like the already modern states of the West and East. Out of this struggle was born the first major theory of development, modernization. According to **modernization theory**, poverty is rooted in domestic or internal deficiencies. These deficiencies might be a lack of capital, poor education, inadequate technology, and attachment to traditional ways of life. It was the job of the Global North to help the Global South overcome these deficiencies by finding money for investment, introducing up-to-date technology, increasing education at all levels, and changing people's values. At this time there was little doubt about what development meant. It meant that "underdeveloped" people should ultimately become more like modern peoples in the West or East. "Underdeveloped" institutions in the Global South would ultimately look like modern institutions in either the West or the East.

In this bipolar world, a Third World country could take one of two directions. If it opted to follow the West, it could jump-start development by fostering free market capitalism, developing business mindsets and habits of hard work, and obtaining financing and technology. As a result, the country could "take off" and then coast rapidly and smoothly along capitalist currents toward an era of high **mass consumption**. Progress would be easy to measure because it was all about how much income people made. Economists measure this progress with **gross domestic product (GDP)**. If GDP rises, life gets better. A large portion of the money to finance these changes would come from foreign aid.

The second choice a country could make was to ally with the USSR, accept the ideology of communism, and adopt strategies for a planned economy. In this case, development would be managed by the heavy hand of the government. The government, with financial and technical assistance from the USSR, would provide education, finances, technology, and managerial expertise, which would lead to the same mass consumption as in the West. Whether Third World countries allied with the US and the West or the USSR and the East, the goal was the same. These countries wanted to create a technologically sophisticated world with improved living standards, longer life expectancy, and more widely distributed wealth.

Those in the West had little doubt that capitalism was the better route to modernization. Its rough edges could be smoothed by an active government. One key role for government was to kick-start the economy without dominating it. This idea grew out of the very successful Marshall Plan for Europe and Japan after World War II. This plan involved lots of aid money for building infrastructure such as roads, power generators, and harbors. The money was also used to finance industrial factories and equipment. Countries in the Third World already had plenty of natural resources – land and minerals. What they did not have was the industrial and infrastructure capacity to take advantage of these resources. By focusing on industrialization, a country could become less dependent on traditional agriculture, workers would move into the cities, and the country's economy would become more productive. Agriculture could also be modernized. Such changes required huge investments that were provided mostly by organizations like the World Bank or by friendly Western governments.

For Christians in the West, it was also easy to choose between the two modernization strategies. Christians, virtually unanimously, preferred the free market approach. To help the Third World, the Christian community supported foreign aid from Western governments that would transfer technology, provide financing for industrial development, and develop infrastructure. In addition, post-World War II Christians were keenly aware of the overwhelming presence of war orphans, refugees, and destitute victims of all sorts. All of these cried out for a compassionate response. In their desire to relieve poverty, Western Christians organized to provide relief to people in need. They sought to respond to the biblical call to provide "a cup of cold water" (Matt. 10:42). Soon after World War II, the Christian community followed the lead of secular organizations like CARE and formed their own organizations to relieve global suffering.

It is no surprise that these organizations often contained the word "relief" in their names. At this time relief was what everyone thought people needed. Christian agencies helped by relieving suffering, while government initiatives promoted the modernization of economies. Here are some still prominent Christian organizations that started up in the two decades after World War II: Catholic Relief Services (1943), World Relief (1944), Lutheran World Relief (1945), Church World Service (1946), World

Had you been alive in the 1950s and 1960s, how might you have responded to global poverty?

World War II is over, and many states in the Third World are now independent. You are distressed by the pictures of children starving in famines around the world. You are afraid of communism. You also doubt Third World countries will be able to develop on their own, so you support the West's efforts to develop their infrastructures and economies. To get more directly involved, you decide to sponsor a child through World Vision. This Christian organization provides relief and is beginning to promote longer term development in places like China, Ghana, and Bangladesh. Working directly with poor people to improve their lives looks promising, and the unjust policies associated with colonialism are being replaced by new policies that emphasize knowledge, technology, infrastructure, and capital. What could go wrong?

Vision (1950), Adventist Development and Relief Agency (1956), and Christian Reformed World Relief Committee (now World Renew, 1962). Many other Christian organizations followed, but these were among the first, and they are still with us.

BASIC NEEDS AND OTHER ATTEMPTS TO FIND A THIRD WAY (1970s)

Many good things were happening in the 1950s and 1960s, and optimism was high. What could go wrong? Sadly, seemingly a lot, for it wasn't long before policymakers realized that Marshall Plan type aid strategies for the developing world weren't working out as well as hoped. Western governments and **international financial institutions** like the World Bank realized that the policies of the 1950s and 1960s actually ignored what was happening in individual countries. Often they imposed strategies that did not take into consideration specific contexts. For example, they forgot to consider unique growing seasons and weather patterns in the tropics. Western policies often worsened income inequality. The money infused at the top did not trickle down to the poor.

As these failures appeared, a broader definition of development emerged. People realized that development was more than industrialization and an increase in a nation's GDP. The very definition of development started to open up. More attention was focused directly on how the lives of the poor were changing. New development theories stressed the importance of meeting people's "basic human needs," especially in the areas of health, education, and nutrition. They also focused attention on the poorest 40 percent of people in the developing world.

Just as Western governments and the World Bank were beginning to realize that their aid efforts were not always effective, the new secular and Christian development organizations were in the process of learning as well. They came to see that relief work isn't always the best approach. All it does is relieve what is hurting at the moment. If people are hungry, it means giving them food. If they are homeless, it means providing them with a safe place to stay. These needs are important to meet after a natural disaster, but organizations discovered that if they just kept giving things out, they created dependency. This dependency was confirmed by the fact that some people seemed to lose their motivation to work to improve their own communities. The realization of this impact led to widespread use of the Chinese proverb, "Give a man a fish, and he will eat for a day. Teach him to fish, and he will eat for a lifetime." Christian organizations moved more into teaching. They taught people how to grow more and better crops, how to improve nutrition, sanitation, and basic health, and how to build more secure homes. Then when the outside organizations left, local communities could tend to their own needs.

US leaders in the 1970s, both in secular and Christian circles, generally thought that capitalism was the best route to development. In the Global South, however, people were not convinced that capitalism was their best choice. When modernization strategies in the 1950s failed to bring about development, they began to consider alternatives. These were often described as "third ways" of development. They were some combination of free markets and government management. Starting in the 1960s, newly independent countries experimented as they struggled to define their path.

In the process, countries in the Global South grew increasingly critical of the World Bank and Western government approaches to development. They argued that the West ignored the structural factors of the global system that were major causes of global poverty. In other words, the playing field favored the rich countries and was tipped against the poor countries of the world. The chief obstacles to development in the Global South were not backward cultural traits, the absence of free markets, or the inability of the governments to promote economic growth. Rather, dependency and extreme poverty were products of historical colonialism, exploitative capitalism, and oppressive **neo-imperialism**. This new approach was called "**dependency theory**." Dependency theory said that Western efforts to pay more attention to the basic needs of the poor were too little and too late. The economically powerful Western countries had not changed their fundamental pro-free market stance. Many in the Global South saw the global economic structures as harmful to them. They argued that these structures, especially in international trade and investment, had to change.

In 1974, countries in the Global South worked through the United Nations General Assembly to produce a document called "The New International Economic Order" (NIEO). The NIEO addressed some necessary structural reforms. For example, **multinational corporations** that had been handled with free market, hands off, policies, would have to be more tightly regulated. Exports from developing countries would receive "**preferential treatment**," which meant lower import tariffs. And foreign aid from the West, which could be used to build infrastructure or other important investments, would be increased.

But the NIEO's policy reforms were never implemented in any significant way. The global economic environment toward the end of the 1970s put the developing world on the defensive. A worldwide recession depressed **commodity prices**, including the price of oil, which hurt Global South economies. More seriously, the heavy economic interventions of governments in the Global South created major problems, including high levels of corruption. The hope that developing countries could put pressure on the West to revise their economic policies and transfer wealth to the Global South evaporated rather suddenly. Additionally, debt burdens in Africa and Latin America became enormous. Rich countries, with economic challenges of their own, were less and less interested in importing the goods that developing countries wanted to export to them. A new era of challenges for development was dawning.

Global poverty is still with us in the 1970s? What do you do?

In the 1970s, the emphasis of the Christian community is on global hunger. Stan Mooneyham of World Vision and Art Simon of Bread for the World have both written compelling books calling Christians to respond to global hunger. At the same time, your confidence in modernization strategies is weakening. You are still worried about communism, but you are pretty convinced that the Vietnam War is a bad deal. You are conflicted. You continue to sponsor children in one of the increasing number of Christian organizations. On the larger scale, you wonder if Christians should rethink their opposition to some of the **insurgencies** around the world.

SAPs,
Socialism, or
Something Else?
(1980s-2000s)

4

THE MARKET AS MARKER OF DEVELOPMENT
(1980s and 1990s)

The elections of Margaret Thatcher in Britain and Ronald Reagan in the US in the 1980s marked a new era in international affairs. There was now less support for government-directed economic plans. Developing countries, via the NIEO, argued that free markets were inherently unfair because they provided a clear advantage to larger and more powerful economic actors. But under the influence of Thatcher and Reagan, policymakers completely disagreed. They believed that reliance on government-directed economic growth was an utter failure and that it was unproductive to favor some industries over others and to subsidize such goods and services as food and transportation. Instead, they argued that the incentives provided by free markets would lead to much better decisions about which industries to invest in. The problem in the developing world was not too much free market, but too little.

The opportunity to promote market-oriented economies came in the form of "**structural adjustment programs**" (SAPs). Under the modernization strategies in vogue after World War II, many countries borrowed heavily and built up huge debts. One reason for this was that during the Cold War, the US encouraged developing countries to borrow investment capital while at the same time encouraging US private banks to lend to friendly Global South governments. Many of these governments borrowed more than they should have. Too often the money went not to good investments, but to line the pockets of those in power. In the early 1980s, the loans came due, and many countries were not able to pay. It was then that the **International Monetary Fund (IMF)** offered to "help" by extending new loans to pay back debts to private banks. But in order to receive the loans, the IMF required developing countries to follow structural adjustment programs.

SAPs were designed to move the countries away from heavy government intervention and toward increasingly private and free markets. To get the loans, indebted countries had to agree to a series of changes. They were required to stop manipulating exchange rates, reduce government deficits, remove price controls, open up import markets, and privatize state-owned enterprises. The hope was that these changes would encourage countries to build up industries that would export more and thus generate greater economic growth. New free market-oriented economies, supported by sound economic policies, would correct the economic sins committed by developing world governments over the previous three decades. The Global South didn't readily accept all these reforms. The changes they required and the austerity they imposed were difficult and painful.

Looming over all these efforts was the dark shadow of the Cold War. It was a reality that influenced all political and economic action in the US. It also hung heavily over the Christian community. Some high profile, progressive Christians met in Switzerland to affirm the Lausanne Covenant, an agreement that affirmed the church's mission to vigorously respond to global poverty. Others, however, worried that focusing too much on the poor smacked of "**socialism**." One voice that prompted concern about global poverty at this time was the book *Rich Christians in an Age of Hunger*, published by theologian Ronald Sider in 1977. Sider pointed out how rich people were in the First World, and contrasted this wealth with how poor the rest of the world was. He cited a host of biblical passages about how important it is for rich Christians to take care of the poor, linking his argument to how unjust our world had become. He concluded by telling his readers what Christians could, and should, do about world hunger and poverty.

Sider especially talked about how the whole international economic system was unfair to the poor. When he studied Scripture, Sider was struck by the structural injustices that both the prophets and Jesus strongly denounced. Sider compared the types of injustice and oppression described in Scripture with those in our modern global economy and found they were the same. He believed that North American prosperity came in part because we had set up a fundamentally unjust system. If we really cared about the poor, charity was not enough. Justice demanded that we change the structures that kept people around the world poor. We would also have to change our way of life. Sider argued that we needed to make our trade laws more fair, increase foreign aid, reform the international system of money, and put controls on global corporations. He also argued that North Americans were consuming too much of the world's resources and that we needed to live more simply. Our Christian faith demanded such actions.

It is likely that Sider's ideas would still be controversial today, but in the late 1970s and early 1980s, they really riled people up. The reality of the Cold War had much to do with this response, although confusion about whether Christians should care for the body as well as the soul also played a role. One harsh reaction was written by David Chilton in 1981, *Productive Christians in an Age of Guilt Manipulators*. Chilton took Sider to task on almost every point, although his basic disagreements are easy to summarize. Yes, the Bible expresses God's continuing love and care for the poor. But the way to help them is not through charity and especially not through government action, which Sider clearly supported. Instead, Chilton argued that if we really want to help, we should focus on bringing the gospel message and on instructing people in biblical principles for managing a good society and economy. By so doing, people would become responsible, hard-working, honest, and productive. They would do all this in a free enterprise system in which the government had a very small role. If we really want to help people around the world, the long term strategy is 1) to evangelize them, and 2) to get them to adopt free market economic systems. In other words, Chilton believed people were poor because they were not Christian and because they hadn't established a biblically based market system. Chilton also inferred that Sider was a closet Marxist and put into doubt whether he was even a Christian. Such was the intensity of this debate prior to 1990.

Being a faithful global Christian in the 1980s.

If you are a world-aware evangelical in the 1980s, you have likely heard about Ron Sider's book, and maybe even read portions of it. Like many, you are suspicious. You are just not convinced by theologians who say that God has a "preferential option for the poor." God sides with all peoples, not just the poor! Still, you wonder about the proxy Cold War battles during this era, like the ones in South Africa and Nicaragua. South Africa is in the news regularly. In fact, on college campuses, activists are putting up shacks to represent the plight of black South Africans living under **apartheid**. They are also urging support for the sanctions campaign. At the same time, you have heard from your friends and family members that the ruling South Africa government is pro-capitalist while the African National Congress aligns itself with the Soviet Union. And besides, if the US imposed sanctions on South Africa, wouldn't sanctions hurt black South Africans more than whites? It's so confusing!

BROADER DEVELOPMENT MODELS
IN THE NEW MILLENNIUM (1990s and 2000s)

In the early 1990s, the global landscape changed again when the Soviet Union collapsed and the Cold War came to an end. For the Global South this made a huge difference. For one thing, there would be no more wars in the Third World in which the US and the USSR supported opposite sides. Also, the US would no longer feel compelled to provide "aid" money to dictators who were US allies, but who didn't seem to care much for the well-being of their own people. With the end of the Cold War, the need for that type of "aid" disappeared.

Liberated from the straightjacket of the Cold War, both the Global North and Global South could now think about development in broader, more holistic terms. New participants could join the discussion without being pigeonholed. Markets could be valued, but also critiqued and improved upon. The role of government could be discussed openly, without participants being judged by ideological litmus tests. Voluntary citizens' organizations, often called civil society, could hold leaders accountable. They could advocate for what they viewed as good policies. Progressives could appreciate the benefits of markets. Conservatives could acknowledge that completely free markets don't always result in the best outcomes or address all the important issues, like education and health.

The end of the Cold War also allowed another increasingly powerful voice from the Global South to be heard. This was the voice that questioned the whole development project. It was labeled "**post-development theory**" because it envisioned a day when the whole idea of "development" would be left behind. This voice asked, "Does everyone want to be rich, industrialized, automated, and generally like the West? Why should we assume this?" Led by anthropologist Arturo Escobar, post-developmentalists believed that "development" had been nothing short of an attack on non-Western people. It had questioned, and at times destroyed, their values, their way of life, their identity, and ultimately their very existence. More than that, the whole language of development and all its associated ideas had been created in the Global North. Voices from the Global South had been completely absent. Thoughtful readers of these views couldn't help but agree that post-developmentalists had a point.

Post-developmentalists proposed alternatives to mainstream development. They encouraged the Global South to take the lead in developing their own communities. A high value was placed on simple living, especially because modern, industrial economies are so environmentally destructive. They encouraged multiple models of economics as well as locally sustainable agriculture practices and cultural protections. Whether or not these alternative structures could work in a globalizing world was a legitimate question. But post-development thinkers made it clear that people everywhere need to be respected, their viewpoints need to be heard, and their votes need to be counted. They insisted that the Global South needed to participate in any decision-making process.

In the new post-Cold War climate at the turn of the millennium, the three main international institutions of global capitalism – the **World Trade Organization**, International Monetary Fund, and World Bank – were also making some key revisions. They were motivated to do so by major and sometimes violent protests. Protesters argued that these institutions were clearly on the side of the rich and against the poor. They pointed to the fact that impoverished states were required to pay back their loans to rich northern banks. Many employees of these organizations were appalled that the protesters had so little basic knowledge of economics. At the same time, they did hear the message the protesters were trying to send. They heard that their programs of harsh austerity, one-size-fits-all models of economic development, and globalized capitalism were not working for many of the world's people.

Winds of change were once again blowing. James Wolfensohn, president of the World Bank from 1995-2005, recognized that the strict modernization approach of economic growth was not working. This led him to two major initiatives. One was the World Faiths Development Dialogue (WFDD), which he initiated in 1998 with George Carey, the Archbishop of Canterbury. This dialogue allowed world development leaders like Wolfensohn to listen to religious leaders who were close to the poor and could represent their hopes for a good life and their understanding of development. Wolfensohn hoped that this dialogue would encourage broader participation in this important conversation. His second initiative was a World Bank project to listen to the poor themselves. The results were published in the book *Can Anyone Hear Us? Voices of the Poor* (2000). The poor who were interviewed for this book surprised the World Bank economists. They highlighted relationships with family and community. These relationships and their religious lives, they said, were every bit as important as economic growth and material goods.

In response to the criticisms, the protests, and what they learned when they stopped to listen, the World Bank and the International Monetary Fund began to emphasize what Marcus Taylor calls a more

> comprehensive approach to development that encompassed not just economic policies but also the institutional, human and physical dimensions of development strategy. These areas range from good governance and the **rule of law**, through to social safety nets, education, health, rural and urban strategies, and environmental and cultural dimensions.

These new ideas in the Global North's broader understanding of development were paralleled by two changes in the Christian community. One was an increasing emphasis on what was called "holistic development." The second was an explosion of short term mission trips among the younger generation of Christians.

For much of the Cold War era, Christians who focused strictly on evangelism were often uncomfortable with all the biblical passages that told them to care for the poor. On the other hand, those who focused more on directly addressing poverty and hunger in the name of Christ didn't always have a clear sense of how the call to share the gospel message came into their work. Now, without the tension of the global struggle to defend the best political and economic system, these two sides were able to come together in a more cooperative environment. Strikingly, some evangelical leaders who had been oriented toward saving souls and bringing people into the church started to see the value of the whole gospel message. Among them was Pastor Rick Warren, author of *The Purpose Driven Life* (2002). He traveled to Rwanda in 2003, witnessed the poverty there, and came to read Scripture with fresh eyes. He noticed that some two thousand biblical passages address poverty and justice for the poor. He responded to his new insights by setting up an organization called the PEACE plan that addresses the needs for reconciliation, education, health, and economic development in the Global South.

Another convert was Richard Stearns, who became president of World Vision US in 1998. He wrote a book called *A Hole in the Gospel* (2009) that lays out how much his views changed. Having been steeped in soul-saving evangelical faith for his whole life, he realized in the 1990s that such an approach "is not the whole gospel. Instead, it's a gospel with a gaping hole." Here is how he sums up his learning: "This gospel – the whole gospel – means much more than the personal salvation of individuals. It means a social revolution." Throughout the rest of the book, Stearns reviews some of those two thousand Bible passages and discusses what they mean for us. Overall, his message is quite consistent with the one Ron Sider presented in 1977, though with less emphasis on the role of the government.

As prominent evangelicals reassessed biblical passages on poverty and urged Christians to become involved with holistic development, younger Christians changed, too. They increasingly began to participate in overseas short term mission (STM) trips. Beginning in the 1990s, churches mobilized young people for "project-based" short term missions in the Global South in order to revitalize youth ministry programming. Travel costs were low, and it was easier to communicate with churches in the Global South. Evangelistic missions and development work used to be the domain of a few. Now they were open to all Christians.

According to Princeton sociologist Robert Wuthnow, "church members in the United States" have "a 20-25 percent likelihood of going on a short-term mission trip."

Some of the youth who participate in these STMs follow up on their experiences by studying international development in college. Casual surveys of students in introductory classes on international development at Christian liberal arts colleges indicate that over half of the students had been on a STM overseas. STMs have motivated younger Christians to become involved with issues of poverty and international development in far more immediate ways than was the case when only a minority of Christians traveled overseas. On the other hand, STMs are sometimes plagued by poor preparation and questionable tactics. Christian development leaders like Steve Corbett and Brian Fikkert have worked to improve STM practice by promoting more intentional short-term mission trips. Instead of simply bringing things into a community from the rich North, STMs should "support long-term development ... focus on the assets of a community, [rather than] focusing on the community's needs", and encourage local community participation in the implementation and evaluation of the STM.

Christians at the turn of the millennium continue to confront global poverty.

As the new millennium arrives, you are thrilled that the Cold War is over. Perhaps now all rich countries will act in unison to help poor countries. The World Bank and the IMF appear to be softening their approach to development, and pastors like Rick Warren and Rob Bell, as well as celebrities like Bono and Angelina Jolie, support projects to alleviate poverty. Your church is organizing a short term mission trip to build a school for poor children in Guatemala. This trip could change lives and bring the gospel to people in a destitute area! But just before you sign up, you read David Livermore's book, *Serving with Eyes Wide Open* (2006). He questions whether short term mission trips are too costly and paternalistic. Will this STM undercut the work of locals and feed the "god-complexes" of all the Americans who are going? You also see an interview on TV with anthropologist Arturo Escobar who argues that Western development projects are exploitative and racist. Whether you listen to Christians or non-Christians, you wonder whether Westerners have any role to play in helping the people in the Global South. Your actions, intentional or not, could well be harmful. Yet poverty around the world is still a problem, and you feel God's call to do something. But what?

So, Should We Help People in the Global South?

5

This journey through the history of development ideas and actions shows us how complex the global situation is. Our understanding of development has broadened, but it has also become more confusing. So many different voices clamor for our attention. Unlike the days right after World War II when modernization was the standard theory and the way ahead seemed clear, now there are many competing views on whether and how to help. Amidst this sea of uncertainty, can we actually help more than hurt people living in the Global South? We believe the answer to this question is a cautious "yes."

It is cautious because international development, like any field, is a work in progress. Failed development projects certainly exist. They should give us pause as we rush out "to help poor people." We also need to be honest with ourselves. The field of international development is steeped in paternalistic assumptions. This is partly due to the original assumption that what we do in the West should be the standard for all people, but it is due also to "bad theology." Christians often assume that certain sectors of life are less tainted by sin than others. Church work and missions, from this perspective, have a leg up on politics and business. And international development is especially blessed by God. How can we hurt the poor, we tell ourselves, if God calls us to this task and if our hearts are in the right place? We've been blessed materially. Shouldn't we bless others? It is this theological narrative, mixed with international development's **Eurocentric** origins, that feed into the "white savior" mentality: the idea that superior and blessed humans (often white) can rescue people of color from their plight.

We must be cautious, then, because international development efforts have a long record of paternalism that has translated into unhelpful and even destructive development projects. We should acknowledge these realities. We should ask forgiveness for supporting development projects that have hurt the poor more than helped. As Christians, we must also repent for believing false theological narratives about our own glorified role in the world.

But this is not the end of the story, and here is where the "yes" comes in. We live in hope because we know about learning and grace. The fact that mistakes in development work have been made and that we've contributed to them shouldn't surprise us. Failures are easy to find in many areas of life, including personal relationships, churches, politics, and business. Why should international development be any different? The real question is whether we learn from our mistakes. We, the authors of this book, are both college professors. We have always tried to do our best in teaching, but of course we have also made many mistakes. Sometimes instead of letting students come to their own reasonable conclusions about things, we tell them what to think. When grading papers, we may focus only on weaknesses rather than pointing out strengths. Other times we overlook opportunities to engage students, disempowering and sometimes even hurting them. But instead of closing the books and quitting, we try to learn from our mistakes, repair broken relationships, and continually create more effective learning environments.

We suggest a similar model of learning and grace for everyone, especially for those engaged in international development work. We can embrace this vocation. We know that we will make mistakes. We know that we are tempted to glorify this field and our own role in it. And we must always be aware of the dangers that come with Western power and privilege in international development. But if we are constantly open to questioning our roles, if we are open to continuous learning, and if we are open to sharing our gifts humbly with others, we will likely contribute to better ways of doing development work. Effective development work can be done. When it happens, just as in effective politics, business, or medicine, we gain a glimpse of the "new heaven and the new earth." In this model of international development work, "helping" out of a sense of superiority, domination, or pity is replaced by serving in solidarity with others.

Bryant Myers, a Fuller Seminary professor and author of the book *Walking with the Poor* (1999), offers a vision of holistic development that has inspired Christians working in development. He reminds us of the full gospel message: God created us to live in relationship with God, other people, creation, and ourselves. All of these relationships are broken. But as Colossians 1 so forcefully says, Christ is the reconciler of "all things." So we must work with Christ to restore *all* of these broken relationships. Spiritual, economic, emotional, social, political, gender, racial, and environmental relationships must all be restored. Myers refers to this approach as "**transformational development**," development of the whole person that focuses on the full life that God intends for all people, here and now and into the eternal future. This can be our focus!

Trends in Development Today

6

One of the ways Christians can contribute to transformational development is by being aware of current trends. We saw in chapters 3 and 4 that much has been learned about what makes a good society and how societies evolve and change. It is true that variations of modernization theory still dominate in many development agencies around the world. But there are alternatives. Instead of focusing on economic growth that somehow trickles down from the top to the masses, the best development strategies now pay a lot more attention to areas of life that are important to people. For example, more direct attention is paid to health, education, environmental sustainability, gender equality, housing, food, security, and peacebuilding than there used to be. Many efforts are directed toward the poorest groups in society. Let's take a look at some of the main trends in development today – trends that promote the broader, more inclusive approaches that have emerged since the 1990s.

INCREASED AID LEVELS AND DEEPENED REFORM: MDGS AND SDGS

We will begin with one of the more well-known approaches, which until 2015 was known as the Millennium Development Goals (MDG) strategy. Initiated in the

United Nations in 2000 and adopted by 189 of the world's countries, this strategy identified eight overarching goals that were to be met by 2015. These goals addressed extreme poverty, universal education, gender equality, child mortality, maternal health, HIV/AIDS, and environmental sustainability. The goals were to be achieved through a global partnership. This strategy was judged by most to be a great success and led in 2015 to the adoption of a new set of seventeen **Sustainable Development Goals** (SDGs) that revise and update the MDGs and especially highlight the need to achieve everything in an environmentally sustainable context. The SDGs will organize efforts through 2030.

It is in the context of the MDGs that the lively contemporary debate about the value of foreign aid was launched by one of the strongest voices for the MDG strategy, economist Jeffrey Sachs. He argued that we know how to eliminate poverty, and we have the necessary resources to do so. It's just a matter of doing it. MDGs could be realized if 1) everyone focused their efforts on the poor themselves, 2) poor country governments invested in education and technology, 3) rich countries held the governments of poor countries accountable, and 4) rich countries came through with more foreign aid. According to Sachs, foreign aid programs failed in the past because they were motivated by Cold War politics instead of a real desire to help. He argued that true foreign aid had hardly been tried, and now was the time to try it. If the West sent long term transformational development aid to countries that really needed it, they could get out of their poverty traps. They would take a step onto what Sachs calls "the first rung of the development ladder."

The MDGs thus represent a new strategy aimed at helping the Global South achieve multiple development goals. The MDGs also emphasized true partnerships between Global North and Global South countries. Global South countries were no longer expected to simply follow the rules imposed on them by Global North countries, as with the structural adjustment programs. Rather, Global South countries worked with Global North countries as full partners. Together they developed poverty reduction plans, and local governments committed more of their own resources to poverty reduction with the increased financial assistance from their partners in the Global North.

Though not all the MDGs were accomplished by 2015, the results were nevertheless stunningly positive. The number of extremely poor people declined from almost two billion in 1990 to a little over 800 million in 2015. Child mortality was cut in half, and maternal mortality was nearly cut in half. More boys and, importantly, more girls enrolled in school. The gains were so significant that Ban Ki-Moon, secretary general of the United Nations, called it "the most successful anti-poverty movement in history."

Why did the MDGs program work so well? One high official in the United Nations identified two reasons. First, the MDGs focused everyone's attention on the people in need, which led governments, development banks, and development agencies to concentrate their policies and programs on these people. Second, the MDGs created a common agenda and led to greater cooperation. Specific outcomes could be achieved in clearly identified areas of need. The hope is that the new SDGs will play a similar role with the similar good results.

PERFORMANCE-BASED AID INITIATIVES AND THE MILLENNIUM CHALLENGE ACCOUNT (MCA)

While the United Nations has been supportive of the MDGs and SDGs, most Global North governments have preferred performance-based aid initiatives. These initiatives send aid to countries with the best track records of alleviating poverty. It makes sense, so the thinking goes, to support governments like Ghana or El Salvador, because these countries have steady economic growth rates and accountable governments. It makes less sense to support the governments of Nigeria or Honduras, because foreign aid to these countries always seems to find its way into the wrong hands. The Millennium Challenge Account (MCA) and the Highly Indebted Poor Countries Initiative (HIPC) are examples of performance-based aid initiatives.

The Millennium Challenge Account, overseen by the Millennium Challenge Corporation (MCC), is a US government managed development fund established by the

US Congress in 2004. It was designed to increase foreign aid by five billion dollars a year to poor countries that are committed to policies that promote development. Receiving countries need to prove their commitment with actual performance in such areas as governing justly, investing in people, and encouraging economic freedom. Overall, a country's performance in seventeen economic and political areas determines whether it receives the money. These areas include civil liberties, political rights, rule of law, trade policy, and fiscal policy.

The MCC insists that countries receiving foreign aid come up with detailed plans for achieving sustainable economic growth and reducing poverty. Countries develop their MCA proposals in consultation with many groups in their society and with MCC teams. The funds are monitored through a local MCC affiliate. This process is both rigorous and transparent.

It is important to point out that the measureable goals and performance evaluations used to award aid are hardly neutral. They are biased toward free market economies and seem to insist on Western models of governance and market development. Supporters suggest that these aid initiatives are the "wave of the future." They have proven track records. One study in 2006 looked at the "MCC effect" and estimated that potential recipient countries improved 25 percent more in the MCC's criteria areas than did other countries. The big problem with the current use of performance indicators is that they are almost always imposed by Global North countries. While the desire for clear indicators of success is completely legitimate, we believe that indicators designed and programs implemented with input from Global South countries, like those evident in the MDGs or SDGs, will bear greater long term fruit.

A GROWING AWARENESS OF THE KEY ROLES THAT WOMEN PLAY

The MDGs, SDGs, and the Millennium Challenge Corporation have taken the explicit inclusion of women very seriously. Women are central to development and the well-being of a whole society. Failure to directly include women leads to tragic consequences, especially for women and girls themselves. Amartya Sen pointed out in 1990 that due to multiple discriminatory practices, 100 million women who should have been living at that time were simply absent from the face of the earth. The recent documentary film "It's a Girl" puts the current figure at 200 million. As Sen and others have demonstrated, this terrible reality results from several practices. Girl fetuses are selectively aborted. Poor families tend to give their scarce food to their boys. Young girls who are married off too early have high mortality rates in childbirth. Women also suffer from domestic violence.

These are all reason enough to pay more explicit attention to the well-being of girls and women, but there are more reasons. The development community has discovered that working directly with women benefits the whole society. Good things happen when we support women's economic opportunities, education, security, health, and political voice. As Muhammed Yunus, founder of Bangladesh's Grameen Bank says, "We noticed that money that goes to families through women brings many more benefits to the family. You can see this in every case. When a man is the borrower, there are some positive changes, but not as many. When women borrow, children become immediate beneficiaries." In 2015, the Christian advocacy organization Bread for the World issued its annual Hunger Report. It was called *When Women Flourish, We Can End Hunger*. It affirmed the points made by Yunus. When development efforts focus on women, children in the home are better fed and healthier overall, they attend school more faithfully and longer, the girls do not marry so young, and domestic violence declines.

It gets even better. Researchers at Brigham Young University recently published *Sex and World Peace* (2012). They argue persuasively that including and empowering women is directly connected to sustainable population growth and improved social conditions. Economic stability and growth improve. Poverty and inequality decline. National security, health, and peaceful living are all improved. This might at first seem surprising, but studies are increasingly showing that these connections are legitimate.

The Grameen Bank in Bangladesh was among the first organizations to target small loans to women. Many other microenterprise organizations, including Christian organizations, have followed the same pattern. One relatively recent innovation in development assistance is "conditional cash transfer programs" that give cash directly to women. Women who receive the cash make certain commitments. For example, they bring their children to health checkups, keep them in school, and resist the temptation to arrange marriages for underage girls. Development organizations large and small, Christian and secular, have learned that women play essential roles in developing and maintaining flourishing societies. These organizations are implementing new women-inclusive programming across the board. There is still much work to be done, so it is important to double down on efforts to empower women throughout the world and through all development programming.

A NEW FOCUS ON PROMOTING BUSINESS

Another big change following the end of the Cold War was the move toward business solutions to poverty. Much early criticism of foreign aid revolved around its support of big and corrupt government bureaucracies and its tendency to create dependency. Conservatives especially did not like the fact that many aid recipients were critical of the free market system. To make development sustainable for the long term, they thought, we need to move toward promoting business solutions. That way people would learn how to be productive, and there would be no need for aid in the long run.

One of the first organizations to move into business promotion was Opportunity International, a Christian organization. Thanks to the uncanny insights of businessman Al Whitaker, Opportunity International started making microloans to small businesses back in 1971, five years before the world-famous Grameen Bank of Bangladesh was started. In the 1980s and 1990s, microfinance really took off. Governmental, multilateral, and **civil society organizations**, many of them Christian, all made microfinance a central part of their programming.

Microfinance and microenterprise are based on the simple idea that providing small loans to poor people helps them either buy the raw materials they need to make something they can sell or to buy something wholesale to sell in a retail market. One person might buy fish at the dock to sell in her town. Another could make an oven and buy the ingredients to make bread. Yet another might buy a used sewing machine to make school uniforms. How can we be sure that people do something worthwhile with their loans and then pay them back? Organizations have learned that women recipients are basically honest to start with. However, when the women are organized into accountability groups, virtually every one repays.

Not convinced that microenterprises would have

enough impact on poverty, some Christian organizations worked to promote small and medium-sized businesses that could hire five to fifty employees. The Mennonite Economic Development Associates (MEDA) and Partners Worldwide both have used this strategy. Their efforts were followed in 2002 by the Business as Mission (BAM) movement that is dedicated to tackling global problems of all sorts through business. In the Cold War era, talking about businesses with a social mission might have been seen as an attack on capitalism, and maybe even a subtle way of encouraging socialism. Now business is increasingly seen as a worthy vehicle for providing jobs, overcoming poverty, and building a sustainable foundation for a thriving community.

A business frame of mind has also become part of a relatively recent approach called "social entrepreneurship." Instead of tackling development issues such as poverty, gender inequality, and health deficits with traditional helping strategies, this new movement focuses on addressing social issues with business solutions. It promotes profit-oriented businesses, yes, but with social purposes. For example, instead of giving away bed nets to fight malaria, social entrepreneurship promotes businesses that 1) make the nets and 2) form marketing networks to distribute the nets where they are in demand. In addition to solving social problems, social enterprises are designed to sustain themselves without constant infusions of donor money.

OWNERSHIP, EMPOWERMENT, AND ADVOCACY

One final trend worth mentioning corresponds to the embrace of good governance. In the 1990s, the World Bank and the IMF highlighted the need for Global South countries to adopt accountable political and legal systems. Good economic policies were not bearing fruit because governments in the Global South were plagued by poorly managed political and legal systems. In some cases, leaders were simply siphoning off revenue through corruption. The solution was to promote accountability and thus reduce corruption and improve government efficiency. Some of the World Bank's funding during this decade supported reform initiatives that strengthened courts, encouraged rule of law, and promoted transparent decision-making.

This agenda, however, was criticized as too Western and neo-imperial. Global North institutions realized they needed to take a backseat to Global South countries that could devise their own economic and political reforms to relieve poverty. So Global South governments were encouraged to shape their own policies. They were urged to develop participatory methods to ensure that all actors within the country – government ministries, members of civil society, business owners, and community members – could voice their opinions. This approach used one of the great lessons learned over the previous decades. Local involvement is essential. Individuals must be empowered to participate. Communities must own their own plans to

reduce poverty and improve their societies. Such ownership was encouraged by requiring countries to write their
own Poverty Reduction Strategy Papers (PRSPs) before
requesting debt relief from the IMF.

Closely linked with the trends of ownership and
empowerment are commitments to the rule of law and
advocacy. Too many communities in the Global South
suffer from systems that ignore or abuse them. How can
people get ahead if the government fails to provide basic
social services like electricity or health care? How can
people improve their lives if government officials demand
bribes in return for letting people sell their goods at market stalls? When governments do not listen to their own
people, everyone, and especially the poor, is injured. The
disease of corruption and the abusive power by unaccount-
able public officials run unchecked. To build a thriving
society, government must be just and run smoothly.

One way to encourage good governance is to support
organizations that investigate and tell the truth about
corruption and lack of accountability. Transparency
International and International Justice Mission are two
organizations that push governments to fight corruption
and lack of accountability. The former is secular and the
latter Christian. Both also advocate for reputable systems
of law and law enforcement. Another key Christian advocacy organization is Bread for the World, which for decades
has lobbied the US government for pro-poor policies. Yet
another is Micah Challenge USA. Micah Challenge urges

churches to advocate before governments and global institutions to end extreme poverty. The new book *Advocating for Justice* (2016), written by five Christian development scholars and practitioners, makes a compelling case for including advocacy as one of our main strategies for building a world in which everyone can flourish.

These organizations and resources are important, but one of their shortcomings is that they are rooted in the Global North. Thus they run the risk of sticking too closely to a Western agenda. Voices of advocacy from the Global South are also vital. Grassroots organizations that aim to redistribute wealth or seriously challenge the status quo, like trade unions or organizations of slum dwellers, bring issues into the development policy debate that must also be taken seriously.

All of these new trends respond to programs that failed or did not work as well as had been hoped. Together they help us realize that if we are willing to take stock of our mistakes, note what has worked, and always focus on learning and improving, we will discover constructive roles to play in working with peoples in the Global South. Over the years, we have come a long way from the simple and naïve approaches of the post-World War II era. In the next chapter, we will review the lessons we have learned and present the stories of two organizations, from among many that could be cited, that are indeed making a positive difference. These stories represent some of the good work that is going on throughout the world.

Two Compelling Stories

7

What have we learned over the last seven decades about helping around the world? It would be impossible to provide a full accounting here of all the lessons that have been incorporated into development work around the globe, but it is possible to capture some of the big ones.

1. Human and social development are about so much more than economics. We used to think that when economies were strong and people had enough money, everything else, like political peace, health, education, and social harmony, would follow. But we have learned that development is more complex and needs to be broader and more holistic.

2. It is important to respect local cultures. Local participation, engagement, ownership, and empowerment are essential. When organizations bring in plans from the outside, making assumptions about what people need and what will help them, development will almost certainly fail.

3. Building on the strengths of people and their countries (often called their assets) is so much more effective than identifying needs and weaknesses and trying to simply fix those.

4. Working relationships, whether they are organizational partnerships or global ventures like the MDGs, flourish when they are cooperative.

5. It is critical to intentionally include the voices of all who are often left out of development programming, women being but one example.

6. Transparency and accountability are essential components of any successful development strategy. Temptations to corruption and abuse of power are strong, which is why power must be limited and people in power constantly watched.

7. We must focus on individuals and local communities, but we must also pay attention to larger structures. Legal systems, the distribution of power, and governing institutions are all part of successful development strategies. We have learned that advocacy is an essential tool for helping those in need.

8. Without an underlying presence of virtue among participants, including commitment, honesty, and trust, the motivation and ability to work together do not arise.

9. For Christians, the guidance of our faith and the lessons of Scripture should help shape our own motivation and models for building a more harmonious world.

These lessons are among those that characterize effective international development. So many successful programs incorporate some or all of these lessons that it was hard to select which organizations to tell you about. We have settled on two that we know quite well. As you read the two stories that follow, try to identify how these lessons have been integrated into the work each organization is doing. You may also want to ask if these lessons have been incorporated into the operation of the organizations you support and to keep them in mind as you vote or advocate before the government. Perhaps they will guide you as you organize your own mission or development program.

WORLD RENEW IN BANGLADESH

World Renew began working in Bangladesh shortly after the country's war for independence from Pakistan in 1971. Bangladesh is one of the world's poorest countries. Almost 170 million people are squeezed into a land mass the size of Wisconsin: 89 percent of the people are Muslim, 10 percent Hindu, and about 1 percent Christian. Half of the people make their living by farming, and the main economic activity in the cities is the garment industry that ships clothes around the world.

Back in 1972, World Renew's first efforts were in agriculture. Gradually they moved toward more comprehensive community development strategies. Like most

non-governmental organizations (NGOs) in the 1970s, World Renew began by providing lots of direct assistance with seeds, fertilizer, and equipment. Soon, however, they became aware of growing dependency and a lack of real internal change. So they moved away from giving goods and resources toward more teaching strategies. In the 1980s, World Renew learned that partnering with local organizations was a much better strategy, and they adopted more of a consultant role. Under this strategy, local partners provided the main energy for programs and projects. These local partners worked much more directly with the people of Bangladesh. World Renew provided training at multiple levels. Sometimes they helped the local partners manage their organizations better. At other times they provided technical training, especially in community development strategies.

One program started in 1990 has grown more and more successful over time. This program forms groups called "people's institutions." These groups are community-based, civil society organizations that together serve almost two hundred thousand members. They work on their own and with government ministries to develop projects that benefit local communities in such areas as health, education, business, and gender equality.

In its early days, the program organized members of local communities into self-help groups. Men and women were organized into separate groups so women could express themselves more freely. Originally the self-help groups focused on saving small amounts of their own income so they could either start microbusinesses or save up for significant expenses. The groups met weekly. It took several years of constant support and encouragement from World Renew's partners, but the groups gradually built trust among themselves. They learned how to select members of good character and developed healthy group dynamics. Over time, the groups became so successful and respected that they spread to other local communities. As they matured, the groups started to think about other issues they could address, and now they send a few of their members to meetings of larger community organizations. The self-help groups, referred to now as "primary groups," also grew organizationally. The initial groups have evolved into three organizational tiers that move upward from the local community to a sub-district to a district, and the district groups are now the official "people's institutions."

Having successfully organized themselves into a large organizational network, these groups have become the structure through which local developmental challenges can be addressed. One specific program carried out through the people's institutions was a six-year health program from 2009-14 that promoted maternal and child health. The main strategy was to train community health volunteers and traditional birth attendants. The training focused on basic knowledge and practices that would help women maintain healthy pregnancies and then take better care of their babies and children. The program had many positive outcomes. Women developed leadership skills. Communities saw better birthing practices and the spread of healthy child care behaviors, such as closely monitoring a child's weight. But among the most tangible outcomes was saving the lives of an estimated 399 children, which included a 36 percent reduction in mortality of children under age five. The provision of government health services also improved due to the professional relationships established between the people's institutions and government offices.

After developing for twenty-five years, the people's institutions are now firmly established, and they make many positive contributions to community life. People regularly come from other parts of Bangladesh and other countries to see this model in action and to learn from it. One powerful component is called "The Learning Circle," which is a monthly meeting of organizations. Here participants share best practices and learn from each other about such important issues as minority land rights and dealing with disabilities. The learning then filters down to the communities.

Key values drive World Renew's work. Showing compassion to people in need is one value. Others include reaching out to the weakest members of the community and treating one's wife kindly and respectfully. World Renew emphasizes treasuring girls as much as boys, being honest with each other, and treating others as valuable human beings. Another value that World Renew brings to its work in Bangladesh is working for peace and justice. They also emphasize gratefulness to God for blessings and improvements in people's lives. World Renew has learned that sometimes the simple kindness and respect that staff members show to colleagues from other religions can have even greater impact than talking about the foundational values of the work.

Much work is yet to be done, but World Renew's development assistance in Bangladesh has been very effective overall. Now check out the story of an organization that focuses more on justice, rule of law, and advocacy.

THE ASSOCIATION FOR A MORE JUST SOCIETY IN HONDURAS

The Association for a More Just Society (AJS), "a Christian organization dedicated to answering God's call to 'act justly,'" was founded in 1998. AJS is involved in matters of public transparency, peace, and security in Honduras, which "is among the poorest countries in Latin America, with 60 percent of its population living in poverty." Honduras is also near the bottom of numerous social indicator lists for the Western hemisphere, such as per capita income, literacy, and life expectancy. Among the main reasons for their troubles are corruption, weak political institutions, and violence, all of which are worsened by the existence of drug trafficking.

AJS was created by individuals who believed that the

poverty reduction efforts of government and civil society organizations in Honduras were insufficient because they did not address the systemic causes of poverty in the country, namely, inadequate laws and unjust actions by those in power. AJS asked questions like, "Can microenterprise loans really aid the poor if property laws are inadequate to support a new business or fixed in favor of the rich and powerful?" or "How can a new school, built by volunteers from a church in the Global North, help address the failing education system that the majority of students rely on?"

AJS's early efforts to combat abuses of power involved advocating for changes in laws related to worker's rights and land rights. Labor rights abuses are common in Honduras. One serious abuse is forced overtime. Workers can put in incredibly long shifts, sometimes over twenty-four hours straight. Other abuses include denying legally mandated pay and arbitrary firing. Since over 25 percent of Hondurans are either unemployed or underemployed, most workers are reluctant to report labor abuses because they fear losing their jobs and even more violent reprisals.

AJS was committed to raising awareness of the plight of these workers. Their Labor Rights project was begun in 2004 with one lawyer on staff. By publicizing labor rights violations, AJS won cases for over 135 individual workers. They also educated over seven thousand workers on their labor rights. Despite these measurable successes, AJS recognized that their strategy of resolving individual cases did little to transform systemic abuse, nor did it change the dismissive attitudes of business managers toward labor rights. Indeed, the tragic assassination of an AJS labor lawyer in 2006 led AJS to conclude that they needed to move from focusing on individual cases of injustice toward strategies that addressed pervasive structural injustice.

One systematic issue impacting the majority of Hondurans is the prevalence of violence. Honduras has one of the highest murder rates in the world. Another problem is a lack of trust in institutions such as courts and security forces that exist to protect people from crime and violence. Nearly 80 percent of Hondurans report having little to no confidence in the court system. Over 80 percent "do not trust Congress or political parties."

In order to build trust in the political system, AJS gradually shifted their focus. AJS continued to advocate for changes in labor and property laws, but they also began to address issues of government oversight and reform, working to expose corruption in and improving the performance of the judicial and security sectors. One of the organizations AJS helped co-found was the Alliance for Peace and Justice, a coalition of civil society organizations that fights rampant corruption by bringing to light abuses of power. AJS has also provided "investigative, legal, and psychological supports for people with few resources who have been victims of violent crime." Interestingly, AJS functions both as critic and helper of the government to carry out its various missions.

AJS has realized measurable success. Over one hundred

perpetrators have been convicted thanks to the strong role AJS has played in helping the prosecution prepare their cases. Greater trust in and respect for the law is clearly emerging in places where AJS is most active. Between 2005 and 2009, the number of homicides nationwide in Honduras nearly doubled from 2,417 to 5,265. By contrast in a neighborhood where AJS worked in the same period, homicides were reduced from forty-two to five. Overall, homicide rates in Honduras have dropped 30 percent in the last three years.

The constructive influence of AJS in Honduras seems only to grow. In 2016, a video came to light that showed leaders of the national police taking money in 2009 to assassinate the Honduran government official charged with fighting the drug traffickers, an assassination that actually took place. These indisputable revelations led the government to get serious about purging the police force of corrupt leaders. The president appointed a three-member commission, two of whom were the advocacy coordinator and a board member of AJS, to "purge and transform" the police force. Remarkably, more than one hundred corrupt officers, nearly 40% of the police leadership, were removed from the force based on the commission's work. Nothing like this has ever happened before in Honduras. AJS's impact on the Honduran system of justice has been significant, and they are now a major force promoting development in Honduras.

A Final
Word

8

We have come a long way since the early days of development work after World War II, a time when most people thought it would not be all that hard to bring people into the joys of modern life.

In recent years, there has been a focus on development projects that don't work. We seem to have jumped to the conclusion that development work everywhere is flawed and destined to cause more harm than good. Christians, despite so many biblical passages that tell us to care for one another, are tempted to give up. Too often we hear an aid cynic citing Jesus' words "you will always have the poor among you" (John 12:8) to justify a lack of concern and blaming the poor for their own problems.

But some among us are not so easily swayed. For starters, Jesus is quoting from the Book of Deuteronomy, where these words are followed by a command; "Therefore I command you to be openhanded toward your fellow Israelites who are poor and needy in your land" (Deut. 15:11). In the New Testament, God's love and our mission are clearly extended to the ends of the earth.

So the real question is not whether we should help our neighbors but how. In the last century, we have been made increasingly aware of global poverty, and we have been on a learning curve since then. But we have learned much, and there are countless development organizations with stories that illustrate effective development work.

The Book of Nehemiah presents another beautiful, powerful development story. Nehemiah laments the poverty of the people who are living in Jerusalem. But he also asks a powerful king for help and willingly leaves his job to work alongside those who are trying to rebuild the protective wall of Jerusalem. Like Nehemiah, we must repent of the role we have played in creating a broken world, and we must lament the poverty and pain that are all around us. Then like Nehemiah, we must follow up with prayer and action. We must advocate before powerful governments, work with people in need, and encourage and include them every step of the way. We must fight off the attacks of those who want to maintain the brokenness and for their own ends keep people around the world in poverty. We must learn as we go, adjusting and changing our strategies as new lessons, new realities, and new needs arise. Like Nehemiah and all those working with him, we must never give up in our efforts to be Christ's servants around the world. We may not be called to rebuild the walls of Jerusalem, but we are called to build a world in which the dignity of everyone is respected, the voice of everyone is heard, and the well-being of everyone is assured.

Notes

Series Editor's Foreword

9 **Midway along the journey of my life:** the opening verse of *The Inferno* by Dante Alighieri, trans. Mark Musa (Bloomington and Indianapolis: Indiana University Press, 1995), 19.

10 **We are always on the road:** from Calvin's 34th sermon on Deuteronomy (5:12-14), preached on June 20, 1555 (*Ioannis Calvini Opera quae supersunt Omnia*, ed. Johann-Wilhelm Baum et al. [Brunsvigae: C.A. Schwetschke et Filium, 1883], 26.291), as quoted by Herman Selderhuis (*John Calvin: A Pilgrim's Life* [Downers Grove, IL: InterVarsity, 2009], 34).

10 **a gift of divine kindness:** from the last chapter of Calvin's French version of the *Institutes of the Christian Religion*. Titled "Of the Christian Life," the entire chapter is a guide to wise and faithful living in this world (*John Calvin, Institutes of the Christian Religion, 1541 French Edition*, trans. Elsie Anne McKee [Grand Rapids: Eerdmans, 2009], 704).

Chapter 1

16 **People often say that the poor are getting poorer:** Information on poverty, drinking water, and child mortality can be found at the United Nations web site on that Millennium Development Goals, http://www.un.org/millenniumgoals/. Data on global slavery can be found at http://www.walkfreefoundation.org/, the site of Australia's

Walk Free Foundation, an organization dedicated to ending modern slavery. Data on refugees comes from the United Nations High Commission on Refugees (UNHCR), http://www.unhcr.org/5672c2576. html. There is no perfect count of the world's street children. The figure of 150 million comes from the United Nations. See http:// www.unesco.org/new/en/social-and-human-sciences/themes /fight-against-discrimination/education-of-children-in-need/ street-children/. An excellent overview of all this progress can be found in Steven Radelet, *The Great Surge: The Ascent of the Developing World* (New York: Simon and Schuster, 2015).

18   **Many recent books argue that when we try to help:** Among these are the following: Dambisa Moyo, *Dead Aid: Why Aid is Not Working and How There is a Better Way for Africa* (New York: Farrar, Straus and Giroux, 2009); William Easterly, *The Tyranny of Experts: Economists, Dictators, and the Forgotten Rights of the Poor* (New York: Basic Books, 2013); and Angus Deaton, *The Great Escape: Health, Wealth, and the Origins of Inequality* (Princeton, NJ: Princeton University Press, 2013).

18   **Recent Christian authors:** Steve Corbett and Brian Fikkert, *When Helping Hurts: How to Alleviate Poverty without Hurting the Poor... and Yourself* (Chicago: Moody Publishers, 2009, 2nd ed., 2012); Robert D. Lupton, *Toxic Charity: How Churches and Charities Hurt Those They Help (And How to Reverse It)* (New York: Harper Collins, 2011). A similar presentation can be found in the documentary film *Poverty, Inc.*, produced by PovertyCure, which is affiliated with the Acton Institute. See http://www.povertyinc.org/.

18   **"Unfortunately, we have also heard some readers":** Corbett and Fikkert, *When Helping Hurts*, 15–16.

19   **... how hard helping really is:** This message, incidentally, is not new. Mainstream evangelicals have been introduced recently to this argument through books like *Toxic Charity* and *When Helping Hurts*, but the argument about paternalistic, even destructive, help has been made by anthropologists, sociologists, political scientists,

and others for many years. To begin an exploration of this literature, see Samir Amin, *Unequal Development* (New York: Monthly Review Press, 1976); Andy Baker, "Race, Paternalism, and Foreign Aid: Evidence from U.S. Public Opinion," *American Political Science Review* 109, no. 1 (2015): 93-109; Arturo Escobar, "Discourse and Power in Development: Michel Foucault and the Relevance of his Work to the Third World," *Alternatives* 10 (1984–1985): 377–400; and Ivan Illich, "Development as Planned Poverty," in *The Post-Development Reader*, ed. Majid Rahnema and Victoria Bawtree, 94–102 (London: Zed Books, 1997).

19   **the best community and national assistance strategies are often different:** One of the more recent ethnographies by China Scherz, *Having People, Having Heart* (Chicago: University of Chicago Press, 2015), unpacks the difference between short term assistance and long term development even more. She discusses the concepts of charity, humanitarianism, and sustainable development, arguing that charity may be better for a community's long term development if it coalesces with cultural norms. Sustainable development, lauded in international development circles, can hurt Global South cultures due to its Western norms and values.

Chapter 2

25   **The world today is divided between what is called the Global North ... and the Global South:** Other classification schemes express a more multi-leveled, economically diverse reality. For example, the World Bank partitions countries into low, middle, and high income groups, with various subcategories within these groups. There are also categories that reference some of the Global South countries that have attained higher economic growth rates, for example emerging economies, the Asian Tigers, and BRICS (Brazil, Russia, India, China, and South Africa).

25   **The history of continuous Global North and Global South interaction:** An overview of the impact of the colonial period on the Global South can be found in Eric Allina-Pisano, "Imperialism and

the Colonial Experience," in *Introduction to International Development*, ed. Paul Haslam, Jessica Schafer, and Pierre Beaudet, 28-44 (Oxford: Oxford University Press, 2009).

26–27 **"in the essential cultural differences"**: Allina-Pisano, "Imperialism and the Colonial Experience," 39.

28 **Though there were exceptions, most Christians supported colonialism**: For a fascinating study of the contribution that colonial era missionaries made to present-day democracy, see Robert D. Woodberry, "The Missionary Roots of Liberal Democracy," *American Political Science Review* 106, no. 2 (2012): 244-74.

Chapter 3

35 **According to modernization theory**: For an overview of modernization theory, see Richard Peet and Elaine Hartwick, *Theories of Development* (New York: Guilford Press, 2009), 103-40. A few primary sources include Samuel Huntington, *Political Order in Changing Societies* (New Haven, CT: Yale University Press, 1968); Seymour Lipset, "Some Social Requisites of Democracy," *American Political Science Review* 53 (1959): 69-105; and Walt Rostow, *Stages of Economic Growth: A Non-Communist Manifesto* (Cambridge: Cambridge University Press, 1960).

35 **If it opted to follow the West, it could jump-start development**: See Marcus Taylor, "The International Financial Institutions," in *Introduction to International Development*, 154-56.

41 **They argued that the West ignored the structural factors of the global system**: David Morrison, "Poverty and Exclusion," in *Introduction to International Development*, 235.

41 **Rather, dependency and extreme poverty**: For an overview of dependency theory, see Peet and Hartwick, *Theories of Development*, 43-96. Primary sources include Samir Amin, "Accumulation and Development: A Theoretical Model," *Review of African Political Economy* 1, no. 1 (1974): 9-26; Fernando Cardoso and Robert Faletto, *Dependency and Development* (Berkeley: University of

California Press, 1979); and Andre Gunder Frank, *Capitalism and Underdevelopment in Latin America* (New York: Monthly Review Press, 1969).

42 **The NIEO addressed**: David Sogge, "The United Nations and Multilateral Actors in Development," in *Introduction to International Development*, 186.

42 **A worldwide recession depressed commodity prices**: Marcus Taylor, "The International Financial Institutions," in *Introduction to International Development*, 159.

Chapter 4

47 **Structural adjustment programs**: For an overview of structural adjustment programs, see Richard Peet and Elaine Hartwick, *Theories of Development* (New York: Guilford Press, 2009), 84-94. See also *Adjustment in Africa: Reforms, Results and the Road Ahead* (Oxford: Oxford University Press, 1994); Kevin Danaher, *Fifty Years is Enough: The Case Against the World Bank and the International Monetary Fund* (Boston: South End, 1999); and Giles Mohan, Ed Brown, Bob Milward, and Alfred Zack-Williams, *Structural Adjustment: Theory, Practice and Impacts* (New York: Routledge, 2000).

49 **One voice that prompted concern about global poverty**: Ronald J. Sider, *Rich Christians in an Age of Hunger: A Biblical Study* (Downers Grove, IL: InterVarsity Press, 1977).

51 **One harsh reaction was written by David Chilton**: David Chilton, *Productive Christians in an Age of Guilt Manipulators: A Biblical Response to Ronald J. Sider* (Tyler, TX: Institute for Christian Economics, 1981).

53 **It was labeled "post-development theory"**: For an overview of post-developmentalism, see Peet and Hartwick, *Theories of Development*, 197-239. Two primary sources include Edward Said, *Culture and Imperialism* (New York: Vintage, 1993) and Wolfgang Sachs, *The Development Dictionary* (London: Zed Books, 1993).

53   **Led by anthropologist Arturo Escobar**: Arturo Escobar, *Encountering Development: The Making and Unmaking of the Third World* (Princeton: Princeton University Press, 1995).

55   **His second initiative was a World Bank project to listen to the poor themselves**: See Deepa Narayan, et al., *Can Anyone Hear Us?: Voices of the Poor* (New York: Oxford University Press for the World Bank, 2000).

55   **"comprehensive approach"**: Marcus Taylor, "The International Financial Institutions," in *Introduction to International Development*, 163.

56   **Among them was Pastor Rick Warren**: See Rick Warren, *The Purpose Driven Life: What on Earth Am I Here For?* (Grand Rapids: Zondervan, 2002) and Timothy C. Morgan, "Purpose Driven in Rwanda: Rick Warren's Sweeping Plan to Defeat Poverty," *Christianity Today* 49, no. 10 (October 2005): 32-36.

56   **Another convert was Richard Stearns**: Richard Stearns, *The Hole in Our Gospel: What Does God Expect of Us?* (Nashville: Thomas Nelson, 2009): 5, 20.

57   **According to Princeton sociologist Robert Wuthnow**: Curt Kruschwitz, "Planning Mission Trips that Matter," in *Traveling Well*, ed. Robert Kruschwitz (Waco, TX: Baylor University Press, 2016), 47. For more statistics related to STMs participation, see Robert Priest, Terry Dischinger, Steve Rasmussen, and C. H. Brown, "Missing or Empty?" *Missiology* 34: 4 (2006): 431-450.

58   **On the other hand, STMs:** See Steve Corbett and Brian Fikkert, *Helping without Hurting in Short Term Missions* (Chicago: Moody Publishers, 2014), 25. See also Noel Becchetti, "Why Mission Trips are a Waste of Time," *The Covenant Companion* (May 2001): 6-10; Randy Friesen, "The Long-Term Impact of Short-Term Missions," *Evangelical Missions Quarterly* 41, no. 4 (2005): 448-54; and Kurt Ver Beek, "The Impact of Short-Term Missions: A Case Study of House Construction in Honduras after Hurricane Mitch," *Missiology* 34, no. 4 (2006): 477-95.

58   Christian development leaders like Steve Corbett and Brian Fik-
      kert have worked to improve STM practice: See Steve Corbett and
      Brian Fikkert, *When Helping Hurts* (Chicago: Moody Publishers,
      2012), 156-60.

59   But just before you sign up: David A. Livermore, *Serving with Eyes
      Wide Open: Doing Short Term Missions with Cultural Intelligence*
      (Grand Rapids: Baker, 2006).

Chapter 5

65   Bryant Myers, a Fuller Seminary professor and author: Bryant L.
      Myers, *Walking with the Poor: Principles and Practices of Transfor-
      mational Development* (New York: Orbis, 1999).

Chapter 6

70   This strategy was judged by most to be a great success: For up-
      to-date information about the SDGs, visit the Sustainable Devel-
      opment Knowledge Platform https://sustainabledevelopment.un
      .org/sdgs.

70   ... was launched by one of the strongest voices for the MDG strat-
      egy: Jeffrey Sachs has written several books promoting the MDGs,
      and now more recently the SDGs. See for example, Jeffrey D. Sachs,
      The End of Poverty: Economic Possibilities for Our Time (New York:
      Penguin Books, 2005) and *The Age of Sustainable Development*
      (New York: Columbia University Press, 2015).

71   They would take a step onto what Sachs calls "the first rung of
      the development ladder." See Jeffrey D. Sachs, *The End of Poverty:
      Economic Possibilities for Our Time* (New York: Penguin Books,
      2005): 18.

71   Ban Ki-Moon... called it "the most successful anti-poverty move-
      ment in history": Ban Ki-Moon makes this comment on page 3
      of *The Millennium Development Goals Report 2015*, published by
      the United Nations. See http://www.un.org/millenniumgoals/2015
      _MDG_Report/pdf/MDG%202015%20rev%20(July%201).pdf.

71   **One high official in the United Nations identified two reasons:**
The official was Olav Kjorven, Assistant Secretary-General and
Director of UNDP's Bureau for Development Policy. See http://www.
undp.org/content/undp/en/home/ourperspective/ourperspective
articles/2011/08/23/why-so-far-the-millennium-development
-goals-have-been-a-success.html.

72   **The Millennium Challenge Account, overseen by the Millennium Challenge Corporation (MCC):** To begin a review of the
MCA, see the Millennium Challenge Corporation's website: https://
www.mcc.gov.

73   **It is important to point out that the measureable goals and
performance evaluations:** Emma Mawdsley, "The Millennium
Challenge Account: Neo-liberalism, Poverty and Security," *Review
of the International Political Economy* 14, no. 3 (2007): 487-509.

73   **One study in 2006 looked at the "MCC effect":** Doug Johnson
and Tristan Zajonc, "Can Foreign Aid Create an Incentive for Good
Governance? Evidence from the MCC," *John F. Kennedy School of
Government* (April 11, 2006): 1-48.

74   **Amartya Sen pointed out in 1990:** See Amartya Sen, "More Than
100 Million Women Are Missing," *New York Review of Books*
(December 20, 1990): 61-66. The website for the "It's a Girl" documentary is http://www.itsagirlmovie.com/.

75   **As Muhammed Yunus... says:** See Muhammed Yunus, "Wom-
en's Empowerment, Microcredit, IT and Poverty," (2013), http://
www.grameen-info.org/womens-empowerment-microcredit-it
-and-poverty/.

75   **It gets even better. Researchers at Brigham Young University:**
See Valerie M. Hudson, Bonnie Ballif-Spanvill, Mary Caprioli, and
Chad F. Emmett, *Sex and World Peace* (New York: Columbia Uni-
versity Press, 2012).

76   **Development organizations large and small:** An excellent overview of the role of women in development can be found in Bread for
the World Institute, *2015 Hunger Report: When Women Flourish...*

We can End Hunger (Washington, DC: Bread for the World Institute, 2014).

77 **One of the first organizations to move into business promotion**: For a brief history of how Opportunity International began, see http://opportunity.org/about-us/history.

78 **... a relatively recent approach called "social entrepreneurship"**: For a good overview of social entrepreneurship, see David Bornstein and Susan Davis, *Social Entrepreneurship: What Everyone Needs to Know* (New York: Oxford University Press, 2010).

79 **Good economic policies were not bearing fruit**: Marcus Taylor, "The International Financial Institutions," in *Introduction to International Development*, 162.

79 **This agenda, however, was criticized as too Western**: Taylor, "The International Financial Institutions," 166-67.

80 **Closely linked with the trends of ownership and empowerment**: David Lewis and Nazneen Kanji, "NGOs and Development: From Alternative to Mainstream?" in *Non-Governmental Organizations and Development* (London: Routledge, 2009): 71-90.

80 **One way to encourage good governance:** Learn more about these four organizations at their web sites: Transparency International http://www.transparency.org/; International Justice Mission (IJM) https://www.ijm.org/; Bread for the World http://www.bread.org/; and Micah Challenge USA http://www.micahchallengeusa.org/.

81 **The new book *Advocating for Justice*:** Stephen Offutt, F. David Bronkema, Robb Davis, Gregg Okesson, and Krisanne Vaillancourt Murphy, *Advocating for Justice: An Evangelical Vision for Transforming Systems and Structures* (Grand Rapids, Baker Academic, 2016).

Chapter 7

87 **World Renew**: The story in this section is based on author interviews with staff members at World Renew as well as two documents. The first is a USAID report titled *Lessons from the*

Ground: A Collection of Case Studies (2015). See https://bangladesh
.savethechildren.net/sites/bangladesh.savethechildren.net/files/
library/Lessons%20from%20the%20Ground%20A%20Collection
%20of%20Case%20Studies.pdf. The second is an evaluation study
requested by USAID in 2014 titled *Final Evaluation: The Healthy
Child and Mother Project* (September, 2014), http://www.mcs
program.org/wp-content/uploads/2015/08/World-Renew-Bangla
desh-FE-Report.pdf.

91   **The Association for a More Just Society:** See AJS's website: http://
www.ajs-us.org/.

91   **Honduras, which "is among the poorest countries in Latin
America":** Giuliana Carducci, Catalina Iglesias, Charlotte Gossett,
Danilo Moura, and Dariela Sosa, "Advocating for Peace, Justice and
Security in Honduras: An Evaluation of *Alianza por la Paz y Justi-
cia*," Transparency International Defense and Security Programme
document (May 2014): 13.

91   **Honduras is also near the bottom of numerous social indicator
lists:** Kurt A. Ver Beek, "A More Perfect Love: Casting Out Fear to
Become Courageous Christians," *Prism* (2010): 20.

92   **AJS was created:** For the description of AJS's founding, see https://
www.ajs-us.org/who-we-are/history.

92   **Labor rights abuses are common in Honduras:** See Gabrielle
Price and Tracy Kuperus, "The Citizen Mobilization Efforts of the
Association for a More Just Society (AJS): A Latin American Case
Study," Paper presented at the Citizen Mobilization in Africa Work-
shop, Stellenbosch, South Africa (July 21, 2014): 1-24.

92   **AJS won cases for over 135 individual workers:** Price and Kuperus, "The Citizen Mobilization Efforts," 10.

93   **Nearly 80 percent of Hondurans report having little to no confidence in the court system:** Carducci, et. al. "Advocating for Peace,"
16.

93   **AJS has also provided "investigative, legal":** Price and Kuperus, "The Citizen Mobilization Efforts," 11.

94   **Between 2005 and 2009, the number of homicides nationwide in Honduras:** Information provided by Katrina Parsons, AJS staff member, 2014-2016. For more information on AJS's efforts at reducing violence, see the paper by Gabrielle Price and Tracy Kuperus or Sonia Nazario, "How the Most Dangerous Place on Earth Got Safer, *New York Times* (August 11, 2016). http://www.nytimes.com/2016/08/14 /opinion/sunday/how-the-most-dangerous-place-on-earth-got -a-little-bit-safer.html.

94   **The constructive influence of AJS in Honduras:** Read more about these developments at https://www.ajs-us.org/content/ corruption-honduras-police-force-and-promise-reform.

Glossary

The definitions used in this glossary were taken from Tracy Kuperus's lecture notes, online dictionaries, or the glossary found in Paul Haslam, Jessica Schafer, and Pierre Beaudet's *Introduction to International Development: Approaches, Actors and Issues* (Oxford: Oxford University Press, 2009). Terms are boldfaced in the text when they first occur.

apartheid: A system of racial discrimination enforced by the National Party of South Africa between 1948 and 1994 under which the rights of black South Africans were removed and the minority rule of whites was maintained.

bipolar world: The situation defining world politics during the Cold War in which two world powers dominated, namely, the United States and the Soviet Union. The two countries held opposing visions for the world.

capitalism: The economic organization of society in which private ownership of property, free markets, and limited government are the norm.

civil society organizations: Civic and social organizations, like church groups, environmental organizations, or women's groups, that are not for profit, voluntarily organized, and independent of the government.

colonialism: A system involving one country settling or occupying territory outside its borders for purposes of economic exploitation or political interests.

commodity prices: Prices associated with the purchase of commodities. Commodities are goods or materials that are exchanged easily in the global marketplace. Examples include agricultural products, fuels, and metals.

communism: The economic organization in which a classless society owns all property collectively and there is a fair distribution of income. Under the Soviet Union, communism was ushered in by the government taking control of the economy and managing it from a centralized planning office.

dependency theory: A theory that explains the origins of poverty, especially in the Global South, by focusing on external factors, in particular the history of colonialism and neo-imperialism. Dependency theorists argue that the economic growth in advanced capitalist states created poverty in the Global South.

dual economy: The existence of two distinct types of economic sectors within an economy. One sector is industrialized, highly productive, globally connected, and profit oriented. The other is agricultural, local, and oriented toward subsistence.

Eurocentric: A focus on the values, practices, and historical development of European culture to the exclusion of others. Often European culture is viewed as superior to all other cultures.

foreign aid: Funds or other aid given to countries with the goal of promoting their economic and social development. Aid can be distributed bilaterally or multilaterally. Bilateral aid is when one country provides aid directly to another country. Multilateral aid involves an institution, like the World Bank, that represents a group of countries and provides aid to individual countries. Foreign aid is also known as foreign assistance, development aid, or international aid.

Global North: A concept used to refer to countries located mainly in the northern hemisphere that are wealthy, politically stable, and internationally powerful. Many of these were the colonizers in the colonial era.

Global South: A concept used to refer to non-industrialized, largely agricultural, poorer nation-states located mainly in the southern hemisphere that, for the most part, were at one time colonized by the states in the Global North.

gross domestic product (GDP): An indicator of economic development that measures the total market value of goods and services in an economy.

indigenous peoples: Peoples who are the original inhabitants of an area or have first-order linguistic and historical ties to a particular region or territory.

insurgencies: Movements by people who feel oppressed and seek to overthrow the ruling authorities. Insurgents use violence and/or political tactics to reach their goals.

international development: A process of change oriented toward overcoming poverty and injustice and promoting health, education, social well-being, and a generally flourishing society in the Global South. Also known as development or sustainable development.

international financial institutions: Financial institutions that have been established by more than one country and are subject to international law. The two international financial institutions that have had the most influence on the Global South's economic development are the International Monetary Fund (IMF) and the World Bank.

International Monetary Fund (IMF): An organization of 189 countries that has a variety of aims, including encouraging global monetary stability, facilitating international trade, promoting sustainable economic growth, and reducing poverty worldwide.

mass consumption: A society of mass consumption is one in which incomes are high, which allows the average level of consumption to be high. The United States is a good example of a mass consumption society.

Millennium Development Goals (MDGs): A set of time-bound and measureable goals and targets for combating poverty, hunger, disease, illiteracy, etc., adopted by world leaders in September 2000 at the United Nations Millennium Summit to be reached by 2015.

modernization theory: A theory that explains the origins of poverty, especially in the Global South, by focusing on deficiencies within countries and how countries can transition to become industrialized, capitalist democracies. For example, Global South countries are poor because they lack access to financial resources, are technologically backward, or are prone to corruption.

multinational corporation: A business that invests across national borders and/or establishes manufacturing facilities or other operations in more than one country. Nike and Shell are examples.

non-governmental organizations (NGOs): Organizations that are engaged in work relating to development or humanitarian issues at local, national, or international levels. Examples include Oxfam, CARE, and World Vision.

neo-imperialism: Indirect economic control of one country by another, especially former colonial powers, to the controlling country's own economic and political advantage.

preferential treatment for imports: Policies that lower tariffs or non-tariff barriers on goods and services imported from preferred countries.

post-development theory: A theory that is highly critical of "the development project," which it argues has been highly destructive of Global South countries and peoples.

rule of law: The principle that laws should govern a country as opposed to the arbitrary whims of individual political figures or groups.

socialism: In traditional Marxist thought, a transitional phase between capitalism and communism. More commonly, a society in which government involvement in the economy to meet social goals is extensive and viewed favorably.

structural adjustment programs (SAPs): A series of economic and social reforms promoted by the World Bank and the International Monetary Fund in the 1980s and 1990s that promoted economic development by minimizing the role of the state and favoring the role of markets.

Sustainable Development Goals (SDGs): A set of 17 development goals agreed upon in 2015 by 190 nations following the completion of the 15-year period during which the Millennium Development Goals (MDGs) were the guiding set of UN-supported development goals.

Third World: During the Cold War, Third World referred to the group of states that fell neither into the Western capitalist camp of the First World nor the Soviet-dominated states of the Second World.

transformational development: An approach to development that seeks positive change in the whole of human life. Although material concerns are important, they are on par with social, spiritual, political, and environmental concerns.

World Bank: A global financial institution that offers loans to Global South countries for the purpose of promoting sustainable economic growth and reducing poverty.

World Trade Organization: A global organization that promotes global trade by helping nations set trade rules and abide by them.

CPSIA information can be obtained
at www.ICGtesting.com
Printed in the USA
LVOW10s2004101217
559295LV00010B/752/P